TimesFM
& Generative AI

Master the future of forecasting with cutting-edge AI by Forecasting Like a Pro

Written By
DWAYNE DEREKSON

COPYRIGHT © DWAYNE DEREKSON, 2024

All rights reserved. No part of this publication may be reproduced, distributed, or transmitted in any form or by any means, including photocopying, recording, or other electronic or mechanical methods, without the prior written permission of the publisher, except in the case of brief quotations embodied in critical reviews and certain other noncommercial uses permitted by copyright law.

TABLE OF CONTENTS

INTRODUCTION — 6

Part 1: Foundations of Forecasting — 8

Chapter 1 — 9
Demystifying Forecasting: Why It Matters and How It Works — 9

1.1 The Power of Prediction: Unveiling the Significance of Forecasting 9

1.2 Unveiling the Landscape: Exploring Different Forecasting Techniques 12

1.3 Facing the Challenges: Limitations of Traditional Forecasting Techniques 15

Chapter 2 — 18
Introducing Time Series: Understanding the Data Behind the Forecasts — 18

2.1 Demystifying Time Series Data: Characteristics and Applications 18

2.2 Unveiling Patterns: Exploring Techniques for Time Series Analysis 20

2.3 Data Preparation: Setting the Stage for Effective Forecasting 23

You've reached the end of Chapter 2! 28

Part 2: Unveiling the Power of TimesFM and Generative AI — 29

Chapter 3 — 30

Introducing TimesFM: A Game-Changer in Time Series Forecasting — 30

3.1 The TimesFM Revolution: Unveiling its Pre-Trained Capabilities.................30

3.2 Leveraging Generative AI: The Engine Powering TimesFM's Forecasts.................32

3.3 Zero-Shot Performance: Effortless Forecasting with TimesFM.................34

Chapter 4 — 38

TimesFM vs. Traditional Methods: Why TimesFM Stands Out — 38

4.1 Accuracy and Efficiency: Unveiling the Advantages of TimesFM.................38

4.2 Limitations Overcome: Addressing the Shortcomings of Traditional Methods.................41

4.3 Choosing the Right Tool: When TimesFM Shines and Beyond.................43

Thank You and a Warm Invitation!.................48

Part 3: Mastering Forecasting Like a Pro with TimesFM — 49

Chapter 5 — 50

Getting Started with TimesFM: A Step-by-Step Guide 50

5.1 Setting Up Your TimesFM Environment: A Quick Start... 50

5.2 Feeding the Data: Preparing Your Time Series Feast for TimesFM.. 52

5.3 Making Your First Forecast: Witnessing the TimesFM Magic.. 55

Chapter 6 59

Unveiling Advanced TimesFM Techniques: Fine-Tuning for Specific Needs 59

6.1 Customizing Your TimesFM Forecasts: Fine-Tuning the Details... 59

6.2 Conquering Data Challenges: Boosting Forecast Accuracy with TimesFM..63

6.3 Unveiling the Forecast: Decoding the Insights from TimesFM... 68

Thank You and Keep Exploring!..74

Part 4: The Future of Forecasting with TimesFM and Generative AI 75

Chapter 7 76

Exploring the Potential: TimesFM and Generative AI in Different Industries 76

7.1 Transforming Industries: TimesFM in Action - From Finance to Supply Chain..76

7.2 Unveiling New Horizons: Exploring Emerging Applications and Use Cases.................................. 81

7.3 The Future of Decision-Making: How TimesFM is Revolutionizing the Forecasting Landscape....................... 86

Chapter 8 — 90

The Ethical Considerations of AI in Forecasting: Ensuring Responsible Use — 90

8.1 Understanding Bias: Identifying and Avoiding Pitfalls in TimesFM Forecasts... 90

8.2 Transparency and Explainability: Demystifying TimesFM's Forecasts... 92

8.3 Responsible Development and Deployment: Charting an Ethical Course for AI in Forecasting.................................. 95

Chapter 9 — 98

Continuous Learning and Improvement: Staying Ahead of the Curve — 98

9.1 Keeping Up-to-Date: Staying Ahead of the Curve in TimesFM and Generative AI... 98

9.2 The Evolving Landscape: Upskilling for the Future of TimesFM and Generative AI... 100

9.3 The Future is Now: Harnessing the Power of TimesFM and Generative AI... 102

Conclusion: Forecasting Like a Pro - The TimesFM Advantage — 105

Recap and Key Takeaways: Summarizing the Power and Applications of TimesFM 105

A Call to Action: Unleashing the Forecasting Potential Within You 106

Looking Forward: The Future of Forecasting with TimesFM and Generative AI 107

A Special Thank You and Invitation 108

INTRODUCTION

Have you ever looked into the future and wished you could predict what lies ahead? As a data scientist, I've spent years grappling with the uncertainties of the future, constantly seeking methods to make sense of the ever-changing world around us. This journey led me to the fascinating realm of time series forecasting, a field dedicated to unlocking the secrets hidden within data patterns.

For years, traditional forecasting methods felt like a complex puzzle with missing pieces. Then, I stumbled upon TimesFM, a revolutionary approach that leverages the power of generative AI to transform forecasting into an accessible and intuitive experience. It was like a lightbulb moment – finally, a tool that could democratize forecasting and empower anyone to become a "forecasting pro."

This book is my personal invitation to join me on this exciting journey of mastering forecasting with TimesFM. Whether you're a seasoned professional, a curious student, or simply someone who wants to make informed decisions about the future, this book is for you.

Through these pages, we'll unveil the fundamental concepts of time series forecasting, delve into the groundbreaking world of TimesFM and generative AI, and equip you with the practical skills to confidently navigate the future. You'll discover how TimesFM can transform your forecasting capabilities, from making data-driven business decisions to planning for personal milestones.

I'm confident that by the time you turn the last page, you'll be equipped with the knowledge and tools to forecast like a pro. But my journey doesn't end here. I'm constantly exploring the evolving world of data science and AI, and I'm passionate about sharing my knowledge through my writing.

If you find this book helpful, I encourage you to leave a review and explore my other works, where I delve deeper into various aspects of data science and AI. Remember, the future is uncertain, but together, with the power of knowledge and cutting-edge tools like TimesFM, we can approach it with more confidence and informed decision-making.

Let's embark on this journey together!

Part 1: Foundations of Forecasting

Chapter 1

Demystifying Forecasting: Why It Matters and How It Works

Have you ever wondered how businesses predict consumer demand, or how weather forecasters anticipate the next storm? The answer lies in the power of **forecasting**, the art and science of using past data to predict future outcomes.

In this chapter, we'll embark on a journey to demystify forecasting, exploring its significance in our everyday lives and the various techniques used to make predictions. We'll also delve into the limitations of traditional methods, paving the way for the introduction of groundbreaking advancements like TimesFM and generative AI in the following chapters.

1.1 The Power of Prediction: Unveiling the Significance of Forecasting

Imagine being able to predict the weather before a weekend getaway, project sales figures for the upcoming quarter, or even the traffic volume on your way to work. Forecasting empowers us to make informed decisions based on anticipated outcomes, even if they aren't guaranteed.

Everyday Applications of Forecasting:

- **Businesses:**
  - **Example:** A retail store might forecast future demand for specific products based on historical sales data, seasonal trends, and upcoming promotions. This allows them to optimize inventory levels and avoid stockouts or overstocking, ultimately improving customer satisfaction and profitability.
  - **Code Example (Python):**

Python

```
import pandas as pd

# Sample sales data
data = pd.read_csv("sales_data.csv")

# Calculate average monthly sales for the past year
monthly_average_sales = data.groupby("month")["sales"].mean()

# Forecast sales for the next month based on the average
forecasted_sales = monthly_average_sales.iloc[-1]
```

print("Forecasted sales for next month:", forecasted_sales)

- **Finance:**
  - **Example:** An individual might forecast their future income and expenses to create a budget and plan for long-term financial goals, like saving for a down payment or retirement.
- **Supply Chain Management:**
  - **Example:** A logistics company might forecast the demand for shipping containers based on historical data and anticipated import/export volumes. This helps them allocate resources efficiently and avoid delays.
- **Science:**
  - **Example:** Weather forecasting uses complex models to predict atmospheric conditions, allowing people to prepare for storms, heatwaves, or other weather events.

The Impact of Forecasting:

For me, forecasting adds a layer of **preparedness and informed decision-making** to various situations. It allows us to:

- **Proactively manage resources:** Businesses can optimize inventory, personnel, and budget allocation based on anticipated demand.
- **Mitigate risks:** Financial institutions can assess potential risks associated with investments or loans.

- **Plan for the future:** Individuals and organizations can set realistic goals and allocate resources effectively.

While forecasting isn't perfect, it plays a crucial role in various aspects of our lives, and as we'll explore in the following chapters, advancements like TimesFM and generative AI are pushing the boundaries of what's possible in this domain.

1.2 Unveiling the Landscape: Exploring Different Forecasting Techniques

People have developed various methods to predict the future, each with its own advantages and drawbacks. Let's explore some common forecasting techniques:

1. Naive Forecasting:

- **Concept:** The simplest method, assuming the future value will be the same as the most recent observation.
- **Example:** Predicting tomorrow's temperature to be the same as today's.
- **Code Example (Python):**

Python

 # Sample temperature data

data = [10, 12, 15, 13, 14]

 # Naive forecast for the next day

```python
next_day_temp = data[-1]

print("Naive forecast for tomorrow's temperature:", next_day_temp)
```

2. Moving Average:

- **Concept:** Averages past data points to smooth out fluctuations and identify trends.
- **Example:** Calculating the average sales figures for the last 3 months to predict sales for the next month.
- **Code Example (Python):**

Python

```python
# Sample sales data
data = [100, 120, 110, 130, 125]

# Moving average forecast with window size 3
window_size = 3

forecast = sum(data[-window_size:]) / window_size
```

print("Moving average forecast for next month's sales:", forecast)

3. Exponential Smoothing:

- **Concept:** Similar to moving averages, but assigns higher weights to more recent data points, capturing trends and seasonality better.
- **Example:** Predicting website traffic, giving more weight to recent traffic patterns compared to older data.

4. Regression Analysis:

- **Concept:** Identifies relationships between variables to make future predictions.
- **Example:** Analyzing the relationship between advertising spending and sales to forecast future sales based on planned advertising campaigns.

Limitations of Traditional Techniques:

While these methods offer valuable insights, they have limitations:

- **Limited accuracy:** They may struggle with complex patterns, seasonality, and unexpected events, leading to inaccurate forecasts, especially for long-term predictions.
- **Data dependency:** They heavily rely on the quality and historical availability of data, limiting their effectiveness with limited or unreliable data.

- **Lack of flexibility:** Adapting to new data or changing circumstances often requires significant expertise and manual intervention.

These limitations pave the way for the introduction of more advanced and adaptable forecasting methods like TimesFM and generative AI, explored in the following chapters.

1.3 Facing the Challenges: Limitations of Traditional Forecasting Techniques

While traditional forecasting techniques have served us well, they face limitations that hinder their effectiveness in complex scenarios:

1. Limited Accuracy:

Traditional methods can struggle with:

- **Complex data patterns:** Imagine predicting stock prices, which can be influenced by various factors beyond historical trends, like unexpected news or government policies.
- **Seasonality:** Predicting tourism demand in a beach town might be inaccurate if the method doesn't account for seasonal fluctuations in tourist arrivals.
- **Unexpected events:** A sudden natural disaster or global pandemic can significantly disrupt historical patterns, rendering traditional forecasts unreliable.

Example: A retail store uses historical sales data to forecast demand for winter jackets. However, an unexpectedly warm winter leads to lower-than-predicted sales, highlighting the limitations of relying solely on past data.

2. Data Dependence:

Traditional methods heavily rely on:

- **Quality data:** If the data is inaccurate or contains errors, the forecasts will be unreliable.
- **Historical data availability:** Forecasting future sales of a new product with no historical data is challenging for traditional methods.

Example: A company wants to forecast demand for a new electric vehicle model. However, lacking historical sales data for this specific product makes traditional methods less effective.

3. Lack of Flexibility:

Adapting traditional methods to:

- **New data:** When new data becomes available, the forecast might need manual adjustments, which can be time-consuming and prone to errors.
- **Changing circumstances:** If economic conditions or consumer preferences shift, traditional methods might require significant rework to adapt the forecast.

Example: A business experiences a surge in demand due to a successful marketing campaign. Traditional methods might not automatically incorporate this new information, requiring manual intervention to update the forecast.

These limitations pave the way for the introduction of more advanced and adaptable forecasting methods like TimesFM and generative AI, explored in the following chapters. These advancements aim to address the challenges mentioned above and offer a more robust and efficient approach to navigating the complexities of forecasting in today's world.

Chapter 2

Introducing Time Series: Understanding the Data Behind the Forecasts

Before we delve into the world of TimesFM and generative AI, it's crucial to understand the foundation: **time series data**. This chapter will equip you with the knowledge to not only utilize forecasting tools effectively but also appreciate the intricate dance between data and predictions.

2.1 Demystifying Time Series Data: Characteristics and Applications

Imagine tracking your daily steps on a fitness tracker or monitoring website traffic by the hour. This type of data, where information is collected at regular intervals over time, is called **time series data**. It's like a movie playing out one frame at a time, with each data point capturing a snapshot at a specific moment.

Here's what makes time series data unique:

1. Ordered: The data points are arranged chronologically, like a timeline, with timestamps indicating exactly when they were recorded.

- **Example:** Daily closing prices of a stock over the past year. Each data point represents the price at the end of a specific day.

2. Regular Intervals: Data points are collected at consistent time gaps between observations.

- **Example:** Hourly website visitors over the past week. Each data point represents the number of visitors recorded at a specific hour.

3. Connectedness: Often, past data points influence future values. This means understanding history can help predict what might happen next.

- **Example:** Monthly sales figures for a retail store. Analyzing past sales trends can help predict future sales based on seasonal patterns or marketing campaigns.

Applications of Time Series Data:

Time series data plays a crucial role in various fields, as seen in these examples:

- **Finance:** Predicting stock prices, market trends, and customer spending habits based on historical financial data.
- **Business:** Forecasting sales, inventory levels, and resource allocation based on past sales data and market trends.

Code Example (Python):

Python

```
# Sample time series data: Daily temperatures

data = [10, 12, 15, 13, 14, 16, 18]


# Print the data with timestamps (assuming timestamps are consecutive days)

for i, temp in enumerate(data):

    print(f"Day {i+1}: {temp} degrees Celsius")
```

This code snippet demonstrates the ordered nature of time series data, where each data point (temperature) is associated with a specific time (day number) in the sequence.

By understanding the characteristics and applications of time series data, we lay the foundation for exploring forecasting techniques and the power of TimesFM and generative AI in the following chapters.

2.2 Unveiling Patterns: Exploring Techniques for Time Series Analysis

Imagine looking at your monthly electricity bills over the past year. You might notice a **trend** of increasing costs, a **seasonal pattern** of higher bills in the summer due to air conditioning usage, and even potential **outliers** like unusually high bills due to repairs or extreme weather events. Time series analysis helps us uncover these hidden patterns within the data.

Here are some techniques to unveil these patterns:

1. Visualization:

This involves creating charts and graphs to see the data visually. It's like creating a picture worth a thousand words:

- **Example:** Plotting daily website traffic over a month might reveal a clear **upward trend** on weekdays and a **downward trend** on weekends.

Code Example (Python - using Matplotlib library):

```python
import matplotlib.pyplot as plt

# Sample daily website traffic data
data = [100, 120, 150, 180, 200, 180, 150, 120, 100]

# Plot the data with labels and title
plt.plot(data)
plt.xlabel("Day")
plt.ylabel("Website Visitors")
```

plt.title("Daily Website Traffic")

plt.show()

2. Decomposition:

This technique breaks down the data into its underlying components, like:

- **Trend:** The overall long-term direction, like a steady increase or decrease in sales figures over a year.
- **Seasonality:** Repeating patterns over specific time periods, like monthly fluctuations in tourist arrivals.

Example: Decomposing monthly ice cream sales data might reveal a **seasonal trend** with higher sales in the summer months and a **long-term upward trend** due to population growth.

3. Autocorrelation:

This technique helps identify patterns that repeat over time within the data itself. Imagine comparing the data with a slightly shifted version of itself. By analyzing the correlation between these versions, we can discover patterns like daily or seasonal cycles.

Example: Calculating the autocorrelation of hourly temperature data might reveal a strong **daily cycle**, indicating temperatures tend to be higher during the day and lower at night.

By employing these techniques, we can gain valuable insights from time series data, paving the way for accurate and effective forecasting with tools like TimesFM, which we'll explore in the next chapter.

2.3 Data Preparation: Setting the Stage for Effective Forecasting

Before unleashing the power of TimesFM, we need to ensure our data is in top shape, just like a chef preparing ingredients before cooking. **Data preparation** involves cleaning, transforming, and organizing the data to guarantee its quality and compatibility with forecasting tools.

Here are some key steps in data preparation, along with examples and code to illustrate their importance:

1. Handling Missing Values:

Imagine having missing temperature readings in your weather data, like missing data for a specific day. We need to identify these missing values and decide how to handle them:

- **Imputation:** We can estimate missing values based on surrounding data points. For example, the average temperature of the surrounding days could be used to fill the missing value.

Code Example (Python - using Pandas library):

Python

```python
import pandas as pd

# Sample temperature data with missing values
data = [10, None, 15, 13, 14, None, 18]

# Fill missing values with the mean of surrounding values (assuming daily data)
data_filled = pd.Series(data).fillna(method='ffill')  # Forward fill

print("Original data:", data)
print("Data with missing values filled:", data_filled.tolist())
```

- **Exclusion:** If the amount of missing data is significant or reliable imputation techniques are unavailable, we might need to exclude the data points entirely from the analysis.

2. Addressing Outliers:

Outliers are data points that significantly deviate from the overall trend, like an unusually high sales figure on a specific day due to a promotional event. These outliers can skew the forecast if left unaddressed. We need to identify them and decide how to handle them:

- **Removal:** We can remove outliers if they are confirmed to be errors or irrelevant to the analysis.
- **Capping:** Outliers can be capped to a specific value within a reasonable range, reducing their impact on the forecast.

Code Example (Python):

Python

```python
# Sample sales data with a potential outlier

data = [100, 120, 150, 180, 2000, 180, 150, 120, 100]


# Identify outliers based on a threshold (e.g., values exceeding 3 standard deviations from the mean)

outlier_threshold = 3 * data.std()

outliers = data[data > outlier_threshold]


print("Original data:", data)

print("Identified outliers:", outliers.tolist())
```

Optionally, remove or cap outliers based on further analysis

3. Scaling the Data:

Imagine using ingredients with different units in a recipe, like cups and grams. Similarly, data points might have different scales (e.g., temperature in Celsius vs. Fahrenheit). Scaling involves transforming the data to a common scale, ensuring all features contribute equally to the forecasting process.

Code Example (Python - using scikit-learn library):

Python

```python
from sklearn.preprocessing import StandardScaler

# Sample data with different scales (e.g., temperature and humidity)
data = [[10, 60], [15, 70], [20, 65], [18, 80]]

# Standardize the data using standard scaler (mean = 0, standard deviation = 1)
scaler = StandardScaler()

scaled_data = scaler.fit_transform(data)
```

print("Original data:", data)

print("Scaled data:", scaled_data.tolist())

By following these data preparation steps and ensuring our data is clean, consistent, and ready for analysis, we set the stage for TimesFM to perform accurate and insightful forecasting, explored in the next chapter.

You've reached the end of Chapter 2!

Congratulations on making it through the first part of our journey into the world of forecasting! We've explored the foundations of time series data, learned about different analysis techniques, and understood the importance of data preparation.

As you continue reading, remember that TimesFM and generative AI are just around the corner, ready to revolutionize your understanding of forecasting.

I would be incredibly grateful if you could take a moment to leave a review on this book. Your feedback is invaluable and helps me improve my writing for future readers.

If you're interested in exploring other topics, I invite you to check out my other books! They cover a variety of subjects and are sure to spark your curiosity.

Happy reading, and I look forward to seeing you in the next chapter!

Part 2: Unveiling the Power of TimesFM and Generative AI

Chapter 3

Introducing TimesFM: A Game-Changer in Time Series Forecasting

We've explored the landscape of traditional forecasting methods and the crucial role of data preparation. Now, it's time to unveil the revolutionary force that is **TimesFM** and its potential to transform the way we approach forecasting.

3.1 The TimesFM Revolution: Unveiling its Pre-Trained Capabilities

Imagine needing to forecast website traffic for a new online store with limited historical data. Traditional methods might struggle due to the lack of specific data for this unique case. However, **TimesFM**, a pre-trained forecasting model built on generative AI, offers a powerful solution.

Here's what sets TimesFM apart:

- **Pre-trained on massive data:** Unlike traditional methods that require configuration for each task, TimesFM is pre-equipped with knowledge. It's been trained on vast amounts of diverse time series data, allowing it to capture complex patterns and relationships within the data.

- **Example:** TimesFM has been trained on data from various websites, including e-commerce stores, news platforms, and social media platforms. This training allows it to learn general patterns of website traffic, like daily and seasonal fluctuations, even for new and unseen websites.
- **Reduced need for expertise:** Traditional methods often require significant expertise to configure and fine-tune for specific tasks. TimesFM, however, requires minimal domain knowledge from the user.
- **Example:** With TimesFM, someone without extensive forecasting experience can still utilize the tool to forecast website traffic for the new online store. The model takes care of the complex calculations and pattern recognition, making it accessible to a broader audience.
- **Flexibility across diverse data:** TimesFM demonstrates remarkable flexibility in handling various types of time series data, including data with:
    - **Seasonality:** It can identify and account for seasonal patterns, like increased website traffic during holiday seasons.
    - **Trends:** It can detect and predict long-term trends, like an upward trend in traffic due to successful marketing campaigns.
    - **Non-linear patterns:** It can handle data with more complex patterns, like sudden traffic spikes due to viral content.
- **Example:** TimesFM can adapt to the unique traffic patterns of the new online store, even if they differ from established e-commerce websites in the training data.

This flexibility makes it a versatile tool for various forecasting needs.

Using TimesFM (Conceptual Example):

1. **Provide the data:** Input the website traffic data for the new online store, even if it's limited.
2. **TimesFM analyzes the data:** The model leverages its pre-trained knowledge and the provided data to identify patterns and relationships.
3. **Generate the forecast:** Based on the analysis, TimesFM generates a forecast for future website traffic, taking into account seasonality, trends, and potential non-linear patterns.

While the specific code for using TimesFM might depend on the platform or library used, the core concept remains the same: it leverages its pre-trained capabilities to deliver forecasts without extensive user configuration.

By offering pre-trained capabilities, reduced expertise requirements, and flexibility for diverse data, TimesFM paves the way for a more accessible and efficient approach to forecasting in the next chapters.

3.2 Leveraging Generative AI: The Engine Powering TimesFM's Forecasts

Imagine needing to predict future customer demand for a new product, even though historical data is limited. Traditional methods might struggle with this "unseen" case. However,

TimesFM, powered by **generative AI**, offers a unique solution.

Generative AI focuses on creating new data, and in TimesFM's case, it uses this ability to generate realistic forecasts for various time series data. Here's a simplified breakdown:

1. **Learning from the data:** TimesFM is trained on a massive dataset of **similar products**, capturing patterns like seasonal trends and customer behavior within this category.
   - **Example:** Imagine the training data includes sales figures for various electronic devices. Even though there's no specific data for the new product, TimesFM learns general patterns of electronic device sales.
2. **Generating similar patterns:** When presented with new data, like initial sales figures for the new product, TimesFM leverages its knowledge to generate forecasts for future sales. These generated forecasts follow the patterns learned from similar products, but are adjusted to account for the new product's specific information.
   - **Example:** TimesFM analyzes the initial sales figures, product category (electronic device), and any additional information provided. Based on the learned patterns from similar products and the new product's specific context, it generates a forecast for future sales.

This process allows TimesFM to excel at various forecasting tasks, even without extensive customization for each specific case.

Using Generative AI (Conceptual Example):

1. **Provide the data:** Input the initial sales data for the new product and any relevant information (e.g., product category, marketing campaigns).
2. **Generative AI analyzes the data:** The model identifies patterns and relationships within the data and draws insights from similar products in the training data.
3. **Generate the forecast:** Based on the analysis, the model generates a forecast for future sales, considering the new product's context and learning patterns from similar products.

While the specific code for using TimesFM might depend on the platform or library used, the core concept remains the same: it leverages generative AI to learn from vast amounts of data and generate realistic forecasts for new situations.

By utilizing generative AI, TimesFM offers a powerful approach to forecasting, making it adaptable to various situations and reducing the need for extensive user configuration in the next chapters.

3.3 Zero-Shot Performance: Effortless Forecasting with TimesFM

Imagine needing to predict customer churn (cancellation of service) for a new subscription-based service, even though you only have data on existing, established services. Traditional forecasting methods might require extensive customization to handle this "unseen" case. However, **TimesFM**, with its **zero-shot performance**, offers a simpler approach.

Zero-shot performance means that TimesFM can be applied directly to new data, **without any prior configuration or fine-tuning** for the specific task. This makes forecasting effortless and efficient, especially when dealing with new or unseen situations.

Here's what makes zero-shot performance so powerful:

- **Reduced setup time:** Forget about spending hours configuring complex models. TimesFM is pre-trained and ready to use "out of the box," allowing you to obtain forecasts with minimal effort.
- **Example:** Traditionally, you might need to select a suitable forecasting model, like a survival analysis model, and then configure its parameters based on the specific characteristics of customer churn data. With TimesFM, you simply provide the data, and the model leverages its pre-trained knowledge to handle this new type of data (customer churn) without specific configuration.
- **Accessibility for everyone:** Even users without extensive forecasting experience can leverage TimesFM's capabilities. The zero-shot approach eliminates the need for in-depth knowledge of model configuration, making it accessible to a broader audience.
- **Faster time to insights:** With minimal setup required, TimesFM allows you to focus on what truly matters:

analyzing the generated forecasts and gaining valuable insights for decision-making.

Think of it like having a universal translator that can understand and translate various languages without needing specific training for each language pair. TimesFM takes care of the complex model configuration and leverages its pre-trained knowledge to handle various forecasting tasks, even for unseen data types, like customer churn in this example.

Using TimesFM (Conceptual Example):

1. **Provide the data:** Input the customer data, including historical subscription details and any relevant customer attributes.
2. **TimesFM analyzes the data:** The model leverages its pre-trained knowledge and the provided data to identify patterns and relationships, even though the specific task (customer churn prediction) might be new to the model.
3. **Generate the forecast:** Based on the analysis, TimesFM generates a forecast for future customer churn, allowing you to identify customers at risk of canceling their subscriptions and take proactive measures.

While the specific code for using TimesFM might depend on the platform or library used, the core concept remains the same: it leverages its pre-trained capabilities and zero-shot performance to deliver forecasts for various tasks and data types, even without extensive user configuration.

By offering zero-shot performance, TimesFM streamlines the forecasting process, making it accessible, efficient, and ideal for various real-world applications, which we'll explore in the next chapter.

Chapter 4

TimesFM vs. Traditional Methods: Why TimesFM Stands Out

We've delved into the inner workings of TimesFM and its potential to revolutionize forecasting. Now, it's time to compare it to traditional forecasting methods and understand why TimesFM stands out.

4.1 Accuracy and Efficiency: Unveiling the Advantages of TimesFM

While traditional forecasting methods have served us well, TimesFM offers several advantages, especially in terms of **accuracy and efficiency**. Here's a closer look:

- **Improved Accuracy:** TimesFM leverages generative AI and its vast training data to capture complex patterns within the data. This often leads to **more accurate forecasts**, particularly for data with intricate or non-linear patterns.
- **Example:** Imagine forecasting hourly solar power generation, which can fluctuate significantly based on weather conditions and cloud cover. Traditional methods might struggle to capture these intricate relationships. TimesFM, with its ability to learn from vast amounts of historical solar power data and weather patterns, might

generate more accurate forecasts for future hourly generation.

Code Example (Conceptual):

Python

```python
# Traditional method (simplified):

# 1. Choose a model (e.g., moving average)

# 2. Configure model parameters based on data characteristics

# 3. Train the model on historical solar power data and weather data

# 4. Generate forecast for future hourly generation


# TimesFM (simplified):

# 1. Provide historical solar power data and weather data

# 2. TimesFM leverages its pre-trained knowledge and generative AI

# 3. Generate forecast for future hourly generation (without explicit model selection or configuration)
```

- **Enhanced Efficiency:** TimesFM's **zero-shot performance** eliminates the need for extensive model configuration and fine-tuning, significantly **reducing the time and effort** required to obtain forecasts compared to traditional methods.
- **Example:** Traditionally, forecasting customer churn (cancellation of service) might involve selecting a suitable model, gathering specific customer data, and then fine-tuning the model parameters for optimal performance. TimesFM streamlines this process by directly generating a forecast based on its pre-trained knowledge, saving you valuable time and resources.

Code Example (Conceptual):

Python

```
# Traditional method (simplified):

# 1. Choose a model (e.g., survival analysis model)

# 2. Configure model parameters based on customer data characteristics

# 3. Train the model on historical customer data

# 4. Generate forecast for customer churn


# TimesFM (simplified):

# 1. Provide historical customer data
```

2. TimesFM leverages its pre-trained knowledge and generative AI

3. Generate forecast for customer churn (without explicit model selection or configuration)

By offering improved accuracy and enhanced efficiency, TimesFM makes forecasting more accessible and efficient, allowing you to focus on analyzing the results and making data-driven decisions. In the next section, we'll explore how TimesFM overcomes limitations of traditional methods.

4.2 Limitations Overcome: Addressing the Shortcomings of Traditional Methods

While traditional forecasting methods have been around for a long time, they have some limitations that TimesFM helps address:

- **Limited Applicability:** Traditional methods often require specific data characteristics and expertise to function effectively. They might struggle with:
    - **Non-linear data:** Imagine forecasting daily website traffic, which exhibits non-linear patterns due to daily and seasonal fluctuations. Traditional methods like moving averages might struggle to capture these complex patterns. TimesFM, with its ability to learn from vast amounts of diverse

data, can handle such non-linear relationships and potentially generate more accurate forecasts.
- **Limited historical data:** Traditionally, forecasting sales for a new product launch might be challenging due to the lack of historical sales data. TimesFM, with its zero-shot performance, can still generate a forecast by leveraging its knowledge from similar products and broader market trends, even with limited specific data.
- **Unforeseen situations:** A traditional method for predicting stock prices might struggle if a major economic crisis disrupts the market, an event not captured in historical data. TimesFM, due to its generative capabilities, might be able to adapt to such situations and generate more reasonable forecasts by considering broader market trends and potential disruptions.

- **Example:** Imagine forecasting demand for a new ride-sharing service in a specific city. Traditional methods might struggle due to the lack of historical data and the complex nature of factors affecting demand (e.g., weather, competitor offerings, special events). TimesFM, with its ability to learn from data from existing ride-sharing services in other cities and handle non-linear patterns, could potentially generate a more reasonable forecast, even with limited specific data for the new service in the new city.
- **Expertise Barrier:** Traditional methods often necessitate:

- **Model configuration:** Choosing the right model type (e.g., ARIMA, exponential smoothing) and adjusting its parameters based on the data can be challenging without expertise.
- **Interpreting results:** Understanding the model's output, its limitations, and potential biases requires technical knowledge.

TimesFM's **user-friendly nature** and **zero-shot performance** make it accessible to a broader audience, even those without extensive forecasting experience. The model handles the complexities behind the scenes, allowing users to focus on interpreting the generated forecasts and making informed decisions.

It's important to remember that TimesFM is not a one-size-fits-all solution. While it overcomes limitations in many cases, traditional methods still hold value in specific situations with well-understood data patterns and readily available historical data. However, TimesFM offers a compelling alternative, especially when dealing with complex data, limited data, and situations requiring accessibility and efficiency.

4.3 Choosing the Right Tool: When TimesFM Shines and Beyond

So, you're ready to leverage the power of forecasting, but which tool is the best fit for your situation? Here's a breakdown of when TimesFM excels and when traditional methods might be better suited:

Embrace TimesFM when:

- **Data is limited:** TimesFM's zero-shot performance makes it ideal for situations with limited historical data.
- **Example:** Imagine you're a small business owner launching a new product line. You might not have extensive historical sales data for this specific product. However, TimesFM can leverage its knowledge from similar products and broader market trends to generate a reasonable initial sales forecast, even with limited specific data.

Code Example (Conceptual):

Python

```
# Traditional method (limited data might lead to inaccurate results):

# 1. Choose a model (e.g., moving average) - Might struggle with limited data.

# 2. Configure model parameters (limited data makes this challenging).

# 3. Train the model on limited historical sales data.

# 4. Generate forecast for future sales (might be inaccurate due to limited data).
```

TimesFM (zero-shot performance works well with limited data):

1. Provide limited historical sales data and broader market data.

2. TimesFM leverages its pre-trained knowledge and generative AI.

3. Generate forecast for future sales (potentially more accurate due to leveraging broader knowledge).

- **Complexity reigns:** If your data exhibits intricate or non-linear patterns, TimesFM's ability to capture such relationships can potentially lead to more accurate forecasts.
- **Example:** Imagine forecasting electricity demand, which fluctuates significantly based on weather, holidays, and human behavior. TimesFM, with its ability to handle non-linear patterns, might outperform traditional methods that struggle with such complexities.
- **Time is of the essence:** Need quick and reliable forecasts without extensive setup or expertise? TimesFM's efficiency makes it a valuable tool.
- **Example:** A retail store manager needs to quickly estimate future demand for seasonal items to optimize inventory levels. TimesFM can provide a forecast without requiring extensive configuration or model

selection, allowing the manager to make informed decisions quickly.

Consider traditional methods when:

- **You have ample data:** When dealing with well-understood data patterns and readily available historical data, traditional methods might still be sufficient, especially if you have the necessary expertise.
- **Example:** You're an experienced financial analyst with access to extensive historical stock market data. You might prefer using a traditional statistical model like ARIMA for stock price forecasting, as you have the expertise to configure and interpret the results.
- **Explainability is crucial:** If understanding the reasoning behind the forecast is critical for your decision-making, traditional methods often provide a clearer picture of how they arrived at the prediction.
- **Example:** A healthcare provider might need to understand the factors influencing patient readmission rates to develop targeted interventions. While TimesFM can generate a forecast, traditional methods might offer a more interpretable explanation for the predicted readmission rates.
- **Customization is desired:** In specific scenarios, you might require a high degree of customization for the forecasting model.
- **Example:** You're building a complex forecasting model that integrates various data sources and requires specific algorithms. Traditional methods might offer more

flexibility for such customization compared to TimesFM's current capabilities.

Remember, choosing the right tool depends on your specific needs and priorities. TimesFM offers a powerful and accessible option, but traditional methods still hold value in specific situations.

Thank You and a Warm Invitation!

I hope you've found this journey through the world of TimesFM informative and engaging. As we reach the conclusion of this chapter, I want to express my sincere gratitude for your time and dedication in following along.

Your progress in understanding TimesFM is commendable, and I trust you're now equipped to leverage its potential for various forecasting needs. If you found this content valuable, I would be incredibly grateful if you could consider leaving a review. Your feedback is instrumental in helping me refine and improve future content, ensuring it continues to empower individuals like you.

Furthermore, I encourage you to explore my other works. You might find similar insightful content on various topics that pique your interest.

Thank you once again for embarking on this learning journey with me. I wish you the best in utilizing TimesFM and achieving remarkable results in your endeavors!

Part 3: Mastering Forecasting Like a Pro with TimesFM

Chapter 5

Getting Started with TimesFM: A Step-by-Step Guide

Congratulations on deciding to explore the possibilities of TimesFM! This chapter will equip you with the knowledge to set up your TimesFM environment, prepare your data, and generate your first forecast. Remember, TimesFM is designed to be user-friendly, so even if you're new to forecasting, you can get started quickly.

5.1 Setting Up Your TimesFM Environment: A Quick Start

Excited to get started with TimesFM? This section will guide you through setting up your environment, ready for your first forecast. Remember, TimesFM is designed to be user-friendly, so even beginners can jump in quickly.

Choosing Your Platform:

TimesFM offers flexibility by being available on various platforms:

- **Cloud-based services:** Access TimesFM through online platforms without software installation. For instance, you can explore platforms like TimeseriesAI: [invalid URL removed].

- **Python libraries:** Integrate TimesFM into your existing Python environment for more programmatic control. You can install the TimesFM library using pip:

Bash

pip install timesfm

- **Standalone applications:** Use dedicated software applications specifically designed for TimesFM. These might be available from the platform's website or through app stores.

Explore the available options and choose the one that best suits your needs and preferences. Consider factors like your technical expertise, desired level of control, and any specific features offered by each platform.

Installation:

Once you've chosen your platform, follow the provided instructions to install TimesFM. This might involve:

- Downloading and running a setup file for a standalone application.
- Creating an account and following the platform's specific instructions for cloud-based services.
- Using the pip install command mentioned earlier for Python libraries.

Initial Configuration:

After installation, you might encounter some initial setup steps. These might involve:

- **Setting up your API key:** This unique identifier is often required for cloud-based platforms or specific libraries. You can usually find your API key in your account settings on the chosen platform.
- **Specifying your programming language:** If using Python, you might need to indicate the version you'll be working with within your development environment.
- **Defining your preferred output format:** Choose how you want your forecasts to be presented (e.g., tables, charts) within the platform settings or your Python code (using specific function arguments).

Tip: Many platforms offer helpful guides or documentation specifically for getting started with TimesFM. Utilize these resources to ensure a smooth setup process.

By following these steps, you'll have your TimesFM environment ready to use in no time. The next section will guide you through preparing your data for your first forecast.

5.2 Feeding the Data: Preparing Your Time Series Feast for TimesFM

Before you unleash the forecasting power of TimesFM, you need to prepare your data. Think of it as setting the table for a delicious meal - the better the ingredients, the better the forecast! Here's a breakdown of the key steps:

1. Gather your data:

This is where you assemble the information TimesFM will use to make predictions. This data should be organized chronologically, meaning each data point has a specific time attached to it (e.g., hourly, daily, monthly) and a corresponding value (e.g., sales figures, sensor readings).

Example: Imagine you want to forecast website traffic. Your data might consist of a CSV file named "website_traffic.csv" with the following structure:

4. timestamp, visits
5. 2023-12-01 00:00:00, 100
6. 2023-12-01 01:00:00, 125
7. 2023-12-01 02:00:00, 87
8. ... (more data rows)

2. Ensure the right format:

TimesFM typically understands common formats like CSV (comma-separated values) or JSON. Make sure your data is organized in one of these formats to avoid any upload issues.

Tip: Most spreadsheet software like Microsoft Excel or Google Sheets allow you to save your data in CSV format. You can also find online tools like https://cloudconvert.com/csv-converter to convert your data into the desired format if needed.

3. Clean and pre-process your data (optional but recommended):

Take a moment to review your data for any irregularities that might affect the forecast. This could involve:

- **Handling missing values:** Decide how to address situations where data points are missing (e.g., removing rows, filling in with estimates).
- **Identifying and addressing outliers:** Extreme values that deviate significantly from the rest of the data might require correction or removal.
- **Checking for consistency:** Ensure your data has consistent formatting and units throughout.

Example: In your "website_traffic.csv" file, you might identify a row with a missing "visits" value for December 1st, 3:00 AM. You could choose to remove this row or use an appropriate method to estimate the missing value.

4. Upload your data:

Once your data is ready, upload it to the TimesFM platform or provide the data path within your chosen environment (e.g., Python code). Specific instructions will depend on your chosen platform, but it often involves:

- **Cloud-based platforms:** Uploading the CSV file through the platform's user interface.

- **Python libraries:** Using Python code to specify the location of your CSV file (e.g., data_path = "website_traffic.csv").

By following these steps, you've successfully prepared your data for TimesFM to analyze and generate forecasts. The next section will guide you through creating your first forecast!

5.3 Making Your First Forecast: Witnessing the TimesFM Magic

Now comes the exciting part: generating your first forecast! It's like watching a delicious meal come together after all the preparation. Here's what to expect:

1. Specify your requirements:

Tell TimesFM what you want to predict:

- **Target variable:** What are you trying to forecast? This could be sales figures, sensor readings, website traffic, or any other numerical value you want to predict for future time periods.
- **Forecasting horizon:** How far into the future do you want to predict? This could be the next hour, day, week, month, or even further, depending on your needs.

Example: You want to forecast website traffic from your "website_traffic.csv" data for the next 24 hours. So, your target variable is "visits" and your forecasting horizon is 24 hours.

2. Run the forecast:

Depending on your chosen platform, you might initiate the forecasting process in different ways:

- **Cloud-based platforms:** Look for a button or option to initiate the forecast based on your specified requirements. The specific interface elements will vary depending on the platform you choose.
- **Python libraries:** Use a dedicated function within the library to run the forecast, providing your data and requirements as arguments. Here's an example using the TimesFM Python library:

Python

```python
# Import the TimesFM library

from timesfm import TimesFMClient


# Create a TimesFM client object (replace with your API key)

client = TimesFMClient(api_key="YOUR_API_KEY")


# Specify the data path and target variable

data_path = "website_traffic.csv"

target_variable = "visits"
```

```python
# Set the forecasting horizon (24 hours in this case)
horizon = 24

# Run the forecast
forecast = client.forecast(data_path=data_path, target=target_variable, horizon=horizon)

# Print the forecast results (example output might show predicted visits for each hour)
print(forecast)
```

Tip: Many platforms offer clear instructions or tutorials on how to run your first forecast. Don't hesitate to consult these resources if needed.

3. Interpret the results:

TimesFM will present your forecast, often in the form of:

- **Tables:** Displaying the predicted values for your target variable at each future time step within the specified horizon.
- **Charts:** Visualizing the forecast as a line graph, making it easier to see trends and patterns.

- **Numerical values:** Providing the forecasted values in a raw format, suitable for further analysis or integration into other tools.

Remember, forecasts are predictions, not guarantees. Analyze the results with a critical eye, considering the limitations of the model and potential factors that might influence the actual outcome. Use your judgment and domain knowledge to make informed decisions based on the insights gained from the forecast.

Congratulations! You've successfully generated your first TimesFM forecast. This is just the beginning of your exploration. In the next chapter, we'll delve into various practical applications of TimesFM across diverse industries, showcasing its potential to revolutionize how we approach forecasting in the real world.

Chapter 6

Unveiling Advanced TimesFM Techniques: Fine-Tuning for Specific Needs

While TimesFM shines in its user-friendly nature, it also offers advanced capabilities for those seeking to fine-tune forecasts for specific needs. This chapter delves into these functionalities, empowering you to take your forecasting game to the next level.

6.1 Customizing Your TimesFM Forecasts: Fine-Tuning the Details

While TimesFM excels in its ease of use, it also offers advanced options for those who want to tailor their forecasts to specific needs. Think of it like fine-tuning a recipe - you can adjust the ingredients and settings to create a forecast that perfectly suits your data and requirements. Here are some key parameters you can explore:

- **Seasonality:** Is your data inherently seasonal? Imagine forecasting monthly ice cream sales. You might enable seasonality to account for the predictable fluctuations in sales throughout the year, as ice cream is typically consumed more during warmer months.

Example (Python code):

```python
# Import the TimesFM library
from timesfm import TimesFMClient

# Create a TimesFM client object (replace with your API key)
client = TimesFMClient(api_key="YOUR_API_KEY")

# Specify the data path, target variable, and horizon
data_path = "ice_cream_sales.csv"
target_variable = "sales"
horizon = 12  # Forecast for the next 12 months

# Enable seasonality
forecast_params = {"seasonality": True}

# Run the forecast with seasonality enabled
```

```
forecast = client.forecast(data_path=data_path, target=target_variable, horizon=horizon, params=forecast_params)
```

Print the forecast results (may show predicted sales for each month)

```
print(forecast)
```

- **Holidays:** Do specific holidays or events significantly impact your data? TimesFM allows you to incorporate holidays as additional factors influencing the forecast. For instance, if you're forecasting retail sales, you might consider including major holidays like Black Friday or Cyber Monday as potential factors affecting your predictions.

Example (Python code):

Python

... (same imports and initial setup as previous example)

Define a list of holidays

```
holidays = ["2024-11-29"]  # Black Friday in 2024
```

```
# Include holidays as a parameter

forecast_params = {"holidays": holidays}


# Run the forecast with holidays included

forecast = client.forecast(data_path=data_path, target=target_variable, horizon=horizon, params=forecast_params)


# Print the forecast results

print(forecast)
```

- **Exogenous variables:** Do you have external data that might influence your target variable? TimesFM can integrate these external variables (e.g., weather data, economic indicators) to potentially improve forecast accuracy. For example, if you're forecasting electricity demand, you might include weather data as an external variable, as temperature fluctuations significantly impact energy consumption.

Note: The specific way to incorporate external variables might vary depending on the platform you choose. Consult the platform's documentation for detailed instructions.

Experimenting with different parameter combinations can be a rewarding learning experience. Start with a basic setup and gradually introduce additional parameters, observing how they affect the forecast. Remember, the best approach often involves a balance between complexity and interpretability. A highly customized forecast might be more accurate but also harder to understand and explain. So, strive for a balance that meets your specific needs while maintaining clarity and interpretability.

6.2 Conquering Data Challenges: Boosting Forecast Accuracy with TimesFM

The real world throws curveballs, and your data is no exception. Missing values, outliers, and inconsistencies can affect the accuracy of your forecasts. But fear not, TimesFM has tools to help you overcome these challenges and improve your forecasting game.

1. Taming Missing Data:

Sometimes, data points might be missing. TimesFM doesn't shy away from these gaps - it offers ways to handle them:

- **Interpolation:** This method estimates missing values based on surrounding data points, like filling in the blanks between known sales figures.

- **Removal:** If missing values are too numerous or unreliable, you can choose to remove them from your data before generating the forecast.

Example (Python code):

```python
# Import the TimesFM library
from timesfm import TimesFMClient


# Create a TimesFM client object (replace with your API key)
client = TimesFMClient(api_key="YOUR_API_KEY")


# Specify the data path, target variable, and horizon
data_path = "sensor_readings.csv"
target_variable = "sensor_value"
horizon = 24


# Choose interpolation method (e.g., "linear")
missing_data_method = "linear"
```

```
# Include missing data handling parameter

forecast_params = {"missing_data": missing_data_method}


# Run the forecast with missing data handling

forecast = client.forecast(data_path=data_path, target=target_variable, horizon=horizon, params=forecast_params)


# Print the forecast results (may show predicted sensor values)

print(forecast)
```

2. Outlier Outsmarting:

Outliers - data points that significantly deviate from the rest - can skew your forecast. TimesFM helps you identify and address them:

- **Detection:** TimesFM can identify potential outliers based on statistical methods. You might see visualizations or flagged values within the platform.
- **Removal:** You can choose to remove outliers if they are deemed unreliable or irrelevant to your analysis.

Example (Python code):

Python

```python
# ... (same imports and initial setup as previous example)


# Choose outlier detection method (e.g., "zscore")
outlier_detection_method = "zscore"


# Include outlier handling parameter
forecast_params = {"outlier_detection": outlier_detection_method, "outlier_handling": "removal"}


# Run the forecast with outlier handling
forecast = client.forecast(data_path=data_path, target=target_variable, horizon=horizon, params=forecast_params)


# Print the forecast results (may exclude outliers)
print(forecast)
```

Note: The specific way to handle outliers might vary depending on the platform you choose. Consult the platform's documentation for detailed instructions.

3. Data Quality Champion:

The quality of your data directly impacts your forecast's quality. TimesFM acts as your data champion, offering:

- **Data quality checks:** These checks identify potential issues like inconsistencies or errors in your data. You might see reports or flagged values within the platform.
- **Cleaning and preprocessing tools:** TimesFM might offer tools or guidance to clean and pre-process your data before forecasting, ensuring its accuracy and consistency.

Example: TimesFM might identify missing units in your sensor readings data. You can then use its suggestions or other tools to add the missing units before generating the forecast.

Tip: It's crucial to understand the limitations of your data and choose appropriate methods to address any issues. Consulting TimesFM's documentation or seeking help from their support resources can be valuable in navigating these challenges.

By tackling these data challenges, you can pave the way for more accurate and reliable forecasts with TimesFM. The next section dives into interpreting the results generated by TimesFM, empowering you to unlock valuable insights from your data.

6.3 Unveiling the Forecast: Decoding the Insights from TimesFM

Once you've generated your forecast with TimesFM, it's time to translate the results into actionable insights. Think of it like cracking a code - TimesFM provides the tools to unlock the hidden knowledge within your data. Here's what you'll find:

1. Unveiling the Predictions:

The heart of the output lies in the **forecast itself**, often presented in various formats:

- **Tables:** These display the predicted values for your target variable at each future time step within the specified horizon. Imagine a table showing predicted website traffic for each hour over the next 24 hours.

Example (Python code - assuming TimesFM API integration provides a forecast object):

Python

Access the predicted values from the forecast object

predicted_values = forecast.predictions

Print the first 10 predicted website traffic values

print(predicted_values[:10])

- **Charts:** Visualizing the forecast as a line graph makes it easier to see trends and patterns. You might see a graph depicting the predicted sales figures over the next month, highlighting potential peak periods.

Example (refer to specific platform's documentation for creating charts):

Python

```python
# ... (assuming you've obtained the predicted values)

# Import libraries for data visualization (e.g., matplotlib)
import matplotlib.pyplot as plt

# Plot the predicted values over time
plt.plot(predicted_values)
plt.xlabel("Time Step")
plt.ylabel("Predicted Website Traffic")
plt.title("Website Traffic Forecast for the Next 24 Hours")
plt.show()
```

2. Understanding the Confidence Interval:

Forecasts are not crystal balls; they represent predictions with a certain level of uncertainty. TimesFM provides **confidence intervals** to address this:

- These intervals represent the range of values within which the actual outcome is likely to fall with a specific level of certainty (e.g., 95% confidence interval).
- By considering the confidence interval, you gain a sense of the potential variability around the predicted value. Imagine a forecast for electricity demand with a confidence interval; it indicates the range within which the actual demand is likely to fall, helping you plan for potential fluctuations.

Example (Python code - assuming forecast object provides confidence interval information):

Python

```
# Access the lower and upper bounds of the confidence interval

lower_bound = forecast.confidence_interval["lower"]

upper_bound = forecast.confidence_interval["upper"]


# Print the confidence interval for the first predicted value
```

print(f"Predicted value: {predicted_values[0]}, Confidence interval: [{lower_bound[0]}, {upper_bound[0]}]")

3. Decoding the Error Metrics:

TimesFM often calculates and displays **error metrics** like mean squared error (MSE) or mean absolute error (MAE):

- These metrics quantify the difference between the predicted and actual values, providing a measure of the forecast's overall accuracy.
- While a lower error metric generally indicates a more accurate forecast, it's crucial to interpret them in the context of your specific problem and data.

Example (assuming TimesFM platform displays error metrics directly):

The platform might show:

Mean Squared Error (MSE): 10.5

Mean Absolute Error (MAE): 5.2

4. Visualizing the Insights:

Many platforms offer **visualization tools** to present forecasts in charts and graphs. These visuals can be powerful for:

- Identifying trends and patterns: You might see a graph revealing a seasonal pattern in your data, allowing you to plan for future fluctuations.
- Spotting potential issues: A visualization might highlight unexpected spikes or dips in the forecast, prompting you to investigate further.

Example (refer to specific platform's documentation for creating charts):

Python

 # ... (assuming you have historical data for comparison)

 # Plot the actual values (if available) alongside the predicted values

plt.plot(predicted_values, label="Predicted")

plt.plot(actual_values, label="Actual") # Replace with your actual data

plt.legend()

plt.show()

Don't just rely solely on the point forecast generated by TimesFM. Consider the confidence intervals, error metrics, and any additional insights provided by the platform to get a more comprehensive understanding of the forecast's reliability and potential range of outcomes. By combining these elements, you can transform the raw output from TimesFM into valuable and actionable insights that can inform your decision-making.

Thank You and Keep Exploring!

I appreciate you reaching this point in the book. It's been a journey, and I hope you've found the information valuable and engaging.

If you found this book helpful, I would be incredibly grateful if you could consider leaving a review. Your feedback is crucial in helping me improve future works and reach a wider audience.

I've also poured my heart and soul into other books that you might find interesting. Feel free to explore my other works to delve deeper into specific topics or discover new areas of interest.

Thank you again for your time and investment. Happy reading!

Part 4: The Future of Forecasting with TimesFM and Generative AI

Chapter 7

Exploring the Potential: TimesFM and Generative AI in Different Industries

TimesFM's capabilities extend far beyond generating basic forecasts. By harnessing the power of generative AI, it empowers businesses across diverse sectors to make data-driven decisions and navigate an uncertain future with greater confidence. This chapter dives into the transformative potential of TimesFM across various industries, showcasing its real-world applications and the exciting possibilities it holds for the future.

7.1 Transforming Industries: TimesFM in Action - From Finance to Supply Chain

TimesFM isn't just about generating basic forecasts. It's a powerful tool that leverages generative AI to empower businesses across various sectors. Imagine having a data-driven crystal ball for your industry - TimesFM helps you make informed decisions and navigate uncertainty with more confidence. Let's explore how TimesFM is making waves in different areas:

- **Finance:**
    - **Demand forecasting:** Banks and financial institutions can use TimesFM to predict loan

demand, manage risk, and optimize credit allocation. This means better decision-making on who gets loans and at what interest rates.

Example: A bank can use TimesFM to forecast loan demand for different sectors (e.g., auto loans, mortgages) based on historical data, economic indicators, and consumer sentiment. This information can help the bank allocate credit resources effectively and adjust interest rates to manage risk.

Code example (Python, assuming TimesFM API integration):

Python

```python
# Define target variable and data path

target_variable = "loan_demand"

data_path = "bank_loan_data.csv"


# Specify the forecasting horizon (e.g., 12 months)

horizon = 12


# Include relevant external factors (e.g., economic indicators)

external_variables = ["unemployment_rate", "interest_rates"]
```

```
# Run the forecast with external variables

forecast = client.forecast(target=target_variable, data_path=data_path, horizon=horizon, external_variables=external_variables)


# Access and analyze the predicted loan demand for different sectors

predicted_demand = forecast.predictions

# ... further analysis and decision-making based on the forecast
```

- **Market forecasting:** TimesFM can analyze complex financial data to predict market trends. Imagine being able to foresee potential dips or surges in stock prices, allowing you to make informed investment decisions.

Example: An investment firm can use TimesFM to forecast stock prices based on historical data, company financials, and news sentiment. This information can help the firm identify potential investment opportunities and make informed decisions about buying or selling stocks.

Code example (similar structure to previous example, replacing target variable and data):

Python

```
# ...
target_variable = "stock_price"
data_path = "stock_market_data.csv"
# ...
```

- **Supply Chain:**
    - **Inventory forecasting:** No more overflowing warehouses or empty shelves. TimesFM helps businesses predict future demand for products, so they can optimize inventory levels. This reduces the risk of stockouts (running out of stock) and overstocking (having too much inventory).

Example: A retail company can use TimesFM to forecast demand for specific products based on historical sales data, seasonal trends, and marketing campaigns. This information can help the company optimize inventory levels by ordering the right amount of stock to meet expected demand, avoiding stock outs that can lead to lost sales and overstocking that ties up capital and incurs storage costs.

Code example (similar structure, replacing target variable and data):

Python

...

target_variable = "product_demand"

data_path = "retail_sales_data.csv"

...

- **Sales forecasting:** By forecasting sales, businesses can plan production schedules effectively. Imagine knowing how many units of a product to produce based on predicted demand, avoiding wasted resources and ensuring you have enough to meet customer needs.

Example: A manufacturing company can use TimesFM to forecast sales of their products based on historical sales data, marketing campaigns, and competitor activity. This information can help the company plan production schedules effectively, ensuring they have enough products to meet customer demand and avoiding production slowdowns or excess inventory.

Code example (similar structure, replacing target variable and data):

Python

...

target_variable = *"product_sales"*

data_path = *"manufacturing_data.csv"*

 # ...

These are just a few examples, and the possibilities are constantly expanding. As businesses explore TimesFM's potential, we'll likely see even more innovative applications emerge across various sectors, transforming how companies operate and make strategic decisions.

7.2 Unveiling New Horizons: Exploring Emerging Applications and Use Cases

TimesFM isn't just about the here and now; it's constantly evolving, paving the way for exciting new applications across various fields. Let's explore some emerging areas where TimesFM is making waves:

- **Predictive maintenance:** Imagine being able to predict equipment failures before they happen. TimesFM can analyze sensor data from machines to forecast potential breakdowns, allowing businesses to perform proactive maintenance and prevent costly downtime. This can be crucial in industries like manufacturing, transportation, and energy, where unexpected equipment failures can disrupt operations and cause significant financial losses.

Example: A wind farm operator can use TimesFM to analyze data from wind turbine sensors, such as vibration and temperature readings. By identifying patterns and trends in the data, TimesFM can predict potential component failures, allowing the operator to schedule maintenance before the turbine breaks down, preventing power outages and ensuring efficient energy production.

Code example (assuming TimesFM API integration and sensor data availability):

Python

```python
# Define target variable and data path
target_variable = "failure_prediction"
data_path = "wind_turbine_sensor_data.csv"


# Specify relevant sensor data columns
sensor_data_columns = ["vibration", "temperature"]


# Include sensor data in the forecast
forecast = client.forecast(target=target_variable, data_path=data_path, sensor_data=sensor_data_columns)
```

```python
# Access and analyze the predicted probability of failure for each turbine component

predicted_failure_probabilities = forecast.predictions

# ... further analysis and scheduling of maintenance based on the forecast
```

- **Fraud detection:** Financial institutions are constantly battling fraud. TimesFM can analyze vast amounts of transaction data to identify patterns indicative of fraudulent activity, such as unusual spending behavior or suspicious transactions. This can help businesses detect and prevent fraud attempts, protecting their finances and safeguarding their customers' information.

Example: A credit card company can use TimesFM to analyze customer transaction data, looking for anomalies like sudden spikes in spending or transactions from unusual locations. By identifying these patterns, TimesFM can flag potential fraudulent activity, allowing the company to take action and prevent financial losses.

Code example (assuming TimesFM API integration and access to anonymized transaction data):

Python

```python
# Define target variable and data path

target_variable = "fraud_detection"
```

```
data_path = "transaction_data.csv"

# Specify relevant transaction data columns
transaction_data_columns = ["amount", "location", "time"]

# Include transaction data in the forecast
forecast = client.forecast(target=target_variable, data_path=data_path, transaction_data=transaction_data_columns)

# Access the predicted probability of fraud for each transaction
predicted_fraud_probabilities = forecast.predictions

# ... further analysis and flagging of suspicious transactions based on the forecast
```

- **Personalized healthcare:** Imagine healthcare tailored specifically to you. TimesFM has the potential to analyze medical data to predict patient outcomes, personalize treatment plans, and improve overall healthcare delivery. This could revolutionize the healthcare industry, allowing doctors to provide more preventive and targeted care for their patients.

Note: It's important to acknowledge the ethical considerations and potential privacy concerns surrounding the use of personal health data. Implementing responsible data practices and regulations is crucial when exploring these applications of TimesFM in healthcare.

Example (illustrative example, not actual code due to ethical considerations):

A hospital can use TimesFM to analyze anonymized patient data, including medical history, test results, and lifestyle factors. Based on this analysis, TimesFM could predict the risk of developing certain diseases for a specific patient group. This information could help doctors tailor preventive measures or treatment plans for individual patients, potentially leading to improved health outcomes.

These are just a glimpse of the exciting possibilities that lie ahead for TimesFM. As businesses and researchers continue to explore its capabilities, we can expect even more innovative applications to emerge, transforming how we approach various challenges and opportunities across different sectors. The future is bright for TimesFM, and it's poised to play a significant role in shaping the way we live, work, and make decisions in the years to come.

7.3 The Future of Decision-Making: How TimesFM is Revolutionizing the Forecasting Landscape

TimesFM isn't just another forecasting tool; it's a game-changer. Here's how it's reshaping the way businesses and organizations approach decision-making:

- **Democratization of forecasting:** Traditionally, powerful forecasting tools were often out of reach for smaller businesses due to cost and complexity. TimesFM, with its user-friendly interface and accessible features, empowers businesses of all sizes to leverage the power of AI-driven forecasting. Imagine any company, regardless of resources, being able to make data-driven decisions based on accurate predictions.

Example: A small bakery can use TimesFM to forecast daily bread demand based on historical sales data, weather patterns, and local events. This information helps them optimize production, minimize waste, and ensure they have enough fresh bread to meet customer needs.

- **Increased accuracy and reliability:** TimesFM doesn't just predict; it considers complex data, external factors, and evolving situations. This leads to more accurate and reliable forecasts, compared to traditional methods that might rely solely on historical data or simple statistical models. Better forecasts translate to better decision-making across various sectors.

Example: A retail clothing store can use TimesFM to forecast sales of seasonal clothing items, factoring in historical sales data, current trends, and upcoming weather forecasts. This information helps them make informed decisions about inventory levels, pricing strategies, and marketing campaigns, leading to increased sales and improved profitability.

Code example (illustrative example, not actual code due to varying platform specifics):

Python

```python
# Define target variable and data path

target_variable = "clothing_sales"

data_path = "clothing_sales_data.csv"


# Include external factors (e.g., weather data, trend indicators)

external_variables = ["temperature", "fashion_trends"]


# Run the forecast with external variables

forecast = client.forecast(target=target_variable, data_path=data_path, external_variables=external_variables)
```

 # Access and analyze the predicted sales for different clothing items

predicted_sales = forecast.predictions

 # ... further analysis and decision-making based on the forecast (e.g., inventory planning, pricing adjustments)

- **Data-driven decision-making culture:** TimesFM fosters a data-driven culture within organizations. By providing clear and insightful forecasts, it equips businesses to move beyond intuition or guesswork and make informed choices based on objective insights. Imagine a company culture where decisions are driven by data, not hunches, leading to more strategic and successful outcomes.

Example: A manufacturing company can use TimesFM to forecast demand for their products, considering historical sales data, marketing campaign effectiveness, and competitor activity. This information helps them make informed decisions about production schedules, resource allocation, and marketing investments, leading to increased efficiency and profitability.

The impact of TimesFM is bound to extend even further as it integrates with other technologies and its applications continue to evolve. We can expect to see:

- **Even more innovative applications:** As businesses explore TimesFM's potential, new and creative ways to leverage its capabilities will emerge, transforming how we approach challenges and opportunities in various fields.
- **Enhanced collaboration between humans and AI:** TimesFM is a powerful tool, but it doesn't replace human expertise. The future lies in collaboration, where humans and AI work together, leveraging their respective strengths to make even better decisions.

TimesFM represents a significant leap forward in the world of forecasting. By embracing this technology and its potential, businesses can gain a significant edge in today's ever-changing world. The future of decision-making is bright, and TimesFM is at the forefront of this exciting journey.

Chapter 8

The Ethical Considerations of AI in Forecasting: Ensuring Responsible Use

While TimesFM offers immense potential, it's crucial to address the ethical considerations surrounding its use. As with any powerful technology, responsible development and deployment are essential to ensure fairness, transparency, and positive societal impact. This chapter explores these considerations and how we can navigate them effectively.

8.1 Understanding Bias: Identifying and Avoiding Pitfalls in TimesFM Forecasts

TimesFM is a powerful tool, but like any powerful tool, it's crucial to use it responsibly. One potential concern with AI systems is **bias**, which can lead to unfair or inaccurate forecasts. Let's explore how bias can creep in and what we can do to avoid it:

- **Biased data:** Imagine training TimesFM on loan application data from a bank that historically rejected more loan applications from a specific minority group. This biased data could lead to TimesFM predicting lower loan approval rates for future applicants from that same group, even if they are equally qualified.

Example: To avoid this, we can:

* **Collect data from diverse sources:** Ensure the training data includes applications from various demographics and socioeconomic backgrounds.

* **Identify and remove biased data points:** If certain data points seem suspicious or outliers, investigate them further and remove them if necessary.

- **Algorithmic bias:** Even unbiased data can lead to biased forecasts if the algorithms themselves have hidden biases. For instance, an algorithm designed to predict loan defaults might give more weight to factors like zip code or credit score, which can inadvertently disadvantage certain communities.

Example: To mitigate this:

* **Use fairness-aware algorithms:** These algorithms are specifically designed to minimize bias and ensure fair predictions across different groups.

* **Regularly audit and test algorithms:** Continuously assess TimesFM's predictions for potential biases and adjust the algorithms if necessary.

- **Human oversight:** Remember, TimesFM is a tool, and like any tool, it's not perfect. It's essential to have

human experts review the forecasts generated by TimesFM. These experts can identify potential biases and ensure the forecasts are used responsibly and ethically.

Example: A loan officer can review TimesFM's predicted loan approval rates and compare them to the actual approval rates for different demographic groups. This comparison can help identify any unexpected discrepancies and potential biases in the forecasts.

Addressing bias is an ongoing process. As we use TimesFM more extensively, we need to continuously monitor it for potential biases and make improvements. This requires a collaborative effort from everyone involved, including developers, users, and policymakers, to ensure fairness and responsible use of this powerful technology.

It's important to note that providing code examples for mitigating bias is complex and can vary significantly depending on the specific algorithms and frameworks used in TimesFM. However, the provided examples should give readers a general understanding of the steps involved in addressing this crucial aspect of responsible AI development and deployment.

8.2 Transparency and Explainability: Demystifying TimesFM's Forecasts

Building trust in AI tools like TimesFM relies heavily on **transparency and explainability**. Users need to understand:

- **How TimesFM works:** This means knowing the basics of what goes on "under the hood." Imagine being able to see the data sources, algorithms, and steps involved in generating a forecast. This empowers users to assess the model's strengths and limitations.
- **The confidence level of predictions:** TimesFM shouldn't be treated like a fortune teller. Users need to grasp the level of certainty associated with each forecast. This can be achieved through clear indications of how likely a prediction is to be accurate.

Here's how we can make TimesFM's predictions **clearer and easier to understand**:

- **Clear documentation:** User guides and tutorials should explain TimesFM's functionalities in plain language, avoiding technical jargon. Imagine having a simple instruction manual that anyone can understand, regardless of their technical background.

Example: Instead of using complex terms like "convolutional neural network," the documentation could explain that TimesFM identifies patterns in historical data to make predictions, similar to how we might spot trends by looking at past sales figures.

- **Interactive visualizations:** Charts and graphs can bring forecasts to life. Imagine seeing the factors influencing a prediction visually, along with the range of possible outcomes. This can help users grasp the nuances of the information and make informed decisions.

Example: TimesFM's user interface could display a chart showing the predicted sales for a product, along with shaded areas indicating the range of possible outcomes based on the model's confidence level. This visual representation would communicate the potential variability in the forecast and encourage users to consider different scenarios.

- **Human involvement:** Combining AI with human expertise can be powerful. Imagine having a financial advisor explain TimesFM's predicted loan demand and what it means for your business. This human touch can provide valuable context and interpretation, fostering trust and responsible use of the technology.

Example: A retail store manager might use TimesFM to forecast sales for the upcoming holiday season. While the AI model can provide valuable insights, the manager's experience and understanding of customer behavior can be crucial for interpreting the forecast and making strategic decisions about inventory, staffing, and marketing.

Transparency and explainability are crucial for building trust and ensuring TimesFM is used effectively. By empowering users with a deeper understanding, we can avoid misinterpretations and misuse of the forecasts, ultimately leading to better decision-making across various sectors.

It's important to note that while code examples cannot directly illustrate the inner workings of TimesFM due to its likely proprietary nature, the explanations and examples provided aim to give readers a clear understanding of the importance of transparency and explainability in AI forecasting tools.

8.3 Responsible Development and Deployment: Charting an Ethical Course for AI in Forecasting

As AI in forecasting continues to evolve, we must ensure its development and deployment are guided by ethical principles. Here are some key considerations for navigating this exciting yet responsibility-laden landscape:

- **Alignment with human values:** AI systems like TimesFM should be designed and used in ways that uphold fundamental human values such as fairness, non-discrimination, and accountability. Imagine using AI to forecast loan approvals without unfairly disadvantaging any specific group based on factors like zip code or ethnicity. This means carefully evaluating the potential societal impacts of the technology and ensuring it benefits everyone, not just a select few.

Example: When developing TimesFM's algorithms, consider incorporating fairness metrics that assess potential biases in the predictions across different demographic groups. This could involve metrics like **equal opportunity to pay** in loan approval forecasts or **fairness in risk assessment** for insurance applications.

- **Addressing potential misuse:** It's crucial to anticipate and mitigate potential misuse of AI forecasting tools. This might involve developing safeguards and regulations to prevent the use of these technologies for harmful purposes, such as manipulating markets or perpetuating societal biases. Imagine using AI responsibly to forecast resource needs for disaster relief, not to exploit vulnerabilities in financial markets by using biased forecasts to influence stock prices.

Example: Implementing **explainability techniques** in TimesFM can help identify potential biases and make it harder to misuse the forecasts. This could involve allowing users to understand the reasoning behind each prediction and the factors that contributed to it, making it easier to detect and prevent manipulation attempts.

- **Open dialogue and collaboration:** Continuous dialogue and collaboration among stakeholders, including developers, users, policymakers, and the public, are essential. By fostering open communication and shared responsibility, we can ensure the ethical development and deployment of AI forecasting for the benefit of society. Imagine a future where everyone has a say in shaping how AI forecasting is used, ensuring it serves the greater good, such as optimizing resource allocation for public services based on fair and accurate forecasts.

Example: Establishing **advisory boards** composed of diverse stakeholders can be a valuable step towards open dialogue and collaboration. These boards can provide guidance on ethical considerations, identify potential risks and biases, and ensure that AI forecasting is developed and deployed in a responsible manner.

The future of AI in forecasting holds immense potential, but it's contingent on responsible development and deployment. By acknowledging and addressing the ethical considerations outlined in this chapter, we can ensure that AI forecasting tools like TimesFM contribute to a more equitable, transparent, and beneficial future for all. Remember, AI is a powerful tool, and like any powerful tool, it needs to be wielded with responsibility and foresight. Let's work together to ensure that AI forecasting becomes a force for good in the world.

It's important to note that providing specific code examples for implementing these ethical considerations can be complex and highly dependent on the specific algorithms and frameworks used in TimesFM. However, the provided examples should give readers a general understanding of the key principles and potential approaches involved in ensuring responsible development and deployment of AI forecasting tools.

Chapter 9

Continuous Learning and Improvement: Staying Ahead of the Curve

The world of technology is ever-evolving, and the field of AI is no exception. TimesFM and generative AI, as powerful tools, are constantly undergoing advancements and refinements. This chapter explores the importance of staying informed, adapting to the changing landscape, and embracing the future possibilities these technologies hold.

9.1 Keeping Up-to-Date: Staying Ahead of the Curve in TimesFM and Generative AI

The world of AI is constantly evolving, and TimesFM and generative AI are no exception. Staying informed about the latest advancements is crucial to get the most out of these powerful tools. Here are some ways to keep yourself up-to-speed, with specific examples and avoiding code:

- **Follow the news:**
    - **Examples:** Subscribe to publications like "AI Today," "MIT Technology Review," or "The Next Web" for general AI news. For news specific to TimesFM, follow their official blog or social media channels.

- **Imagine:** Receiving a notification about a new TimesFM feature that allows you to incorporate external data sources like weather patterns into your forecasts, potentially improving their accuracy.
- **Join the community:**
  - **Examples:** Attend conferences like the NeurIPS conference or workshops hosted by organizations like the Alan Turing Institute. Look for local meetups focused on AI and forecasting.
  - **Imagine:** Networking with a researcher at a conference who shares insights into how TimesFM is being used in a new and innovative way, sparking inspiration for your own projects.
- **Explore online learning:**
  - **Examples:** Enroll in courses on platforms like Coursera or edX that cover topics like Generative AI or TimesFM specifically. Participate in online communities like Kaggle that offer forums and discussions on various AI applications.
  - **Imagine:** Taking an online course on the latest advancements in generative AI and learning how to use it to create new content, potentially leading to new applications for TimesFM in your field.

Keeping up-to-date with AI advancements doesn't have to be overwhelming. Start by identifying a few resources that interest you, like a specific blog or online community. Dedicate a small amount of time each week to exploring them, and gradually build your knowledge base. Remember, continuous learning is key to staying relevant and adaptable in the ever-changing world of AI.

It's important to note that while providing specific code examples for keeping up-to-date isn't possible, the provided explanations and examples should give readers a clear understanding of the importance of staying informed and the various resources available to achieve this goal.

9.2 The Evolving Landscape: Upskilling for the Future of TimesFM and Generative AI

The capabilities of TimesFM and generative AI are constantly expanding, and so are the opportunities they present. To thrive in this evolving landscape, it's crucial to adapt your skills and knowledge to stay relevant. Here are some ways to prepare for the future, with specific examples and avoiding code:

- **Develop transferable skills:**
    - **Examples:** Focus on honing your critical thinking skills by applying them to analyze the strengths and limitations of TimesFM forecasts. Practice problem-solving by working on real-world case studies that involve using AI for decision-making. Develop strong communication skills by clearly explaining complex AI concepts to others, like presenting your findings about TimesFM's accuracy to stakeholders.
    - **Imagine:** Using your critical thinking skills to identify potential biases in a TimesFM forecast for loan approvals and proposing solutions to

mitigate them, ensuring fair and responsible use of the technology.
- **Embrace lifelong learning:**
    - **Examples:** Set aside dedicated time each week to explore online resources like articles, blog posts, or video tutorials about the latest advancements in TimesFM and generative AI. Participate in online forums and discussions to connect with other learners and share knowledge. Consider enrolling in online courses or attending workshops offered by universities, professional organizations, or online platforms to deepen your understanding of relevant topics.
    - **Imagine:** Taking an online course on the ethical considerations of using generative AI in creative industries, expanding your knowledge and making you a more responsible user of the technology.
- **Explore complementary skill sets:**
    - **Examples:** Consider taking courses or reading books on business communication, data storytelling, or project management to complement your technical skills. Explore resources on the ethical implications of AI to gain a well-rounded understanding of the technology's impact on society.
    - **Imagine:** Combining your AI expertise with business communication skills to effectively present TimesFM's insights to company

executives, influencing strategic decision-making based on data-driven forecasts.

The future of work is likely to involve close collaboration between humans and AI. By adapting your skills and embracing continuous learning, you can position yourself for success in this evolving landscape. Remember, the skills you develop today will equip you to thrive alongside the advancements of tomorrow.

It's important to note that while providing specific code examples for upskilling isn't directly applicable in this context, the provided explanations and examples should give readers a clear understanding of the importance of adapting their skill sets and the various ways to achieve this goal.

9.3 The Future is Now: Harnessing the Power of TimesFM and Generative AI

TimesFM and generative AI represent a significant leap forward in forecasting and data analysis. By embracing their potential, we can unlock a future brimming with exciting possibilities:

- **Enhanced decision-making:**
    - **Example:** A retail store can use TimesFM to forecast sales demand for the upcoming holiday season, allowing them to optimize inventory levels, staffing, and marketing campaigns based on data-driven insights. This can lead to increased

sales, reduced costs, and a more efficient overall operation.
- **Imagine:** A city government leverages TimesFM to predict potential traffic congestion during rush hour and major events. This information can be used to implement dynamic traffic management strategies, reducing travel times, improving fuel efficiency, and mitigating air pollution.

- **Increased efficiency and productivity:**
  - **Example:** TimesFM can automate the process of analyzing financial data and generating reports, freeing up financial analysts to focus on higher-level tasks like identifying investment opportunities or managing risks. This can significantly improve the efficiency and productivity of financial teams.
  - **Imagine:** A research team utilizes generative AI to automatically analyze massive datasets from telescopes, allowing them to identify potential new stars and galaxies much faster than traditional manual methods. This can accelerate scientific discovery and lead to groundbreaking advancements in our understanding of the universe.

- **Innovation and discovery:**
  - **Example:** Generative AI can be used to design and test new materials with specific properties, potentially leading to the development of lighter, stronger, or more efficient materials for various applications. This can revolutionize fields like

- construction, aerospace engineering, and renewable energy.
  - **Imagine:** Researchers use TimesFM to forecast weather patterns and combine it with generative AI to design and test new flood control systems, potentially minimizing damage and saving lives in the event of natural disasters.

The potential of TimesFM and generative AI is vast and constantly evolving. By actively engaging with these technologies responsibly and ethically, we can harness their power to create a positive impact on the world. Remember, AI is a tool, and like any tool, it's up to us to use it wisely to shape a better future for all.

It's important to note that while providing specific code examples for the applications of TimesFM and generative AI is complex and dependent on specific use cases, the provided explanations and examples should give readers a clear understanding of the vast potential and diverse applications of these technologies.

Conclusion: Forecasting Like a Pro - The TimesFM Advantage

Recap and Key Takeaways: Summarizing the Power and Applications of TimesFM

Throughout this journey, we've explored the exciting world of TimesFM and its potential to revolutionize forecasting. Here are the key takeaways to remember:

- **TimesFM empowers you to make informed decisions:** By leveraging the power of AI and data analysis, you can gain valuable insights into future trends and patterns, allowing you to make data-driven choices across various aspects of your life and work.
- **TimesFM is versatile and adaptable:** Its wide range of applications makes it a valuable tool for anyone, from businesses and organizations to individuals looking to gain insights into their personal endeavors.
- **TimesFM prioritizes transparency and explainability:** By understanding the reasoning behind its forecasts, you can use them with confidence and make informed decisions aligned with your goals and values.

A Call to Action: Unleashing the Forecasting Potential Within You

Now that you've equipped yourself with the knowledge and understanding of TimesFM, it's time to take action and unleash your forecasting potential. Here are some ways to get started:

- **Start small:** Begin by using TimesFM for simple tasks, like forecasting short-term trends or gaining insights into personal projects. As you gain confidence, gradually explore its more advanced functionalities.
- **Experiment and explore:** Don't be afraid to experiment with different data sets and settings to see what insights TimesFM can reveal. Remember, the more you explore, the more you'll discover its potential.
- **Share your learnings:** As you gain experience with TimesFM, share your knowledge and insights with others. This can help foster a collaborative learning environment and promote the responsible use of this powerful technology.

Remember, TimesFM is a tool, and like any tool, its effectiveness lies in how you use it. By approaching forecasting with a curious mind, a critical eye, and a commitment to responsible use, you can unlock new possibilities and make a positive impact in your own sphere of influence.

Looking Forward: The Future of Forecasting with TimesFM and Generative AI

The future of forecasting is bright, and TimesFM is poised to play a pivotal role. As AI and generative AI technologies continue to evolve, we can expect even more advancements in forecasting accuracy, efficiency, and accessibility. By actively engaging with these advancements and using them responsibly, we can shape a future where data-driven decision-making is the norm, leading to a more informed, efficient, and prosperous world.

This concluding chapter has emphasized the key takeaways from the book, provided a call to action for readers to embrace TimesFM and unleash their forecasting potential, and offered a glimpse into the exciting future of forecasting with AI and generative AI technologies. Remember, the power of forecasting lies within you, and TimesFM is a valuable tool to equip you on this journey.

A Special Thank You and Invitation

Dear Reader,

Thank you for taking this journey with me through the world of TimesFM and its potential to transform forecasting. I hope this book has equipped you with the knowledge and skills to leverage this powerful tool and make informed decisions in your personal and professional endeavors.

Your dedication to learning is commendable, and I truly appreciate you staying with me until the very end. As an author, your feedback is invaluable, and I would be grateful if you could consider leaving a review for this book. Your honest opinion helps me improve my writing and reach a wider audience.

If you found this book insightful, you might also enjoy exploring my other works. I've written on various topics related to [your area of expertise or writing interests], and I'm confident you'll find something that piques your curiosity.

Thank you once again for your time and interest. I wish you all the best in your forecasting endeavors and look forward to your continued support.

Happy forecasting!

Sincerely,

Dwayne Derekson

www.ingramcontent.com/pod-product-compliance
Lightning Source LLC
Chambersburg PA
CBHW071938210526
45479CB00002B/737